Fossils Give Us Clues

by Maribeth Boelts

The dinosaurs lived a long, long time ago. How do people know what dinosaurs looked like?

3

People look at fossils to find out.

5

Most fossils are made of stone.

7

When animals died long ago, some sank into mud.

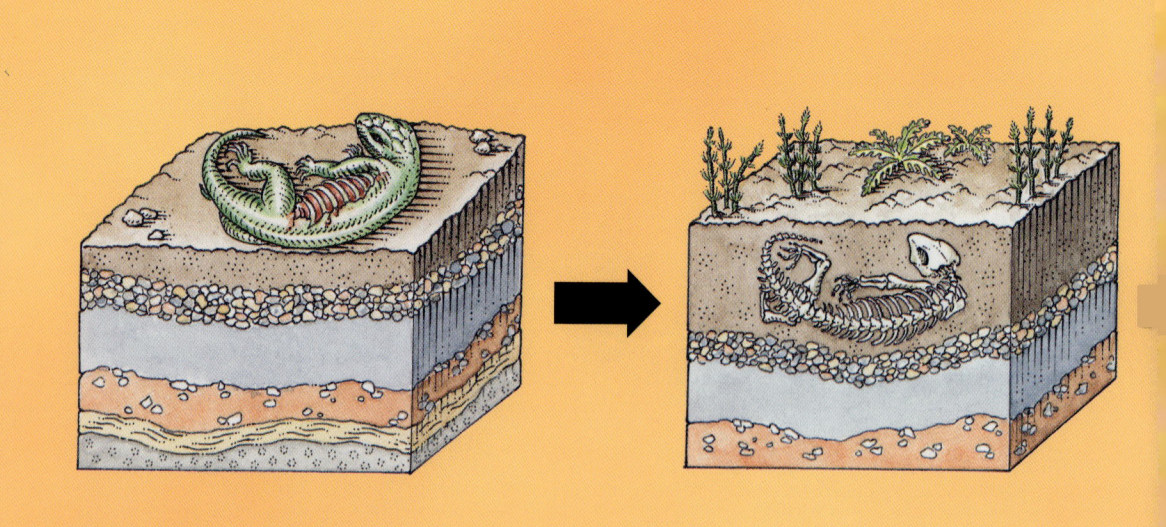

The mud turned into stone. The animals' bones and teeth turned into stone, too.

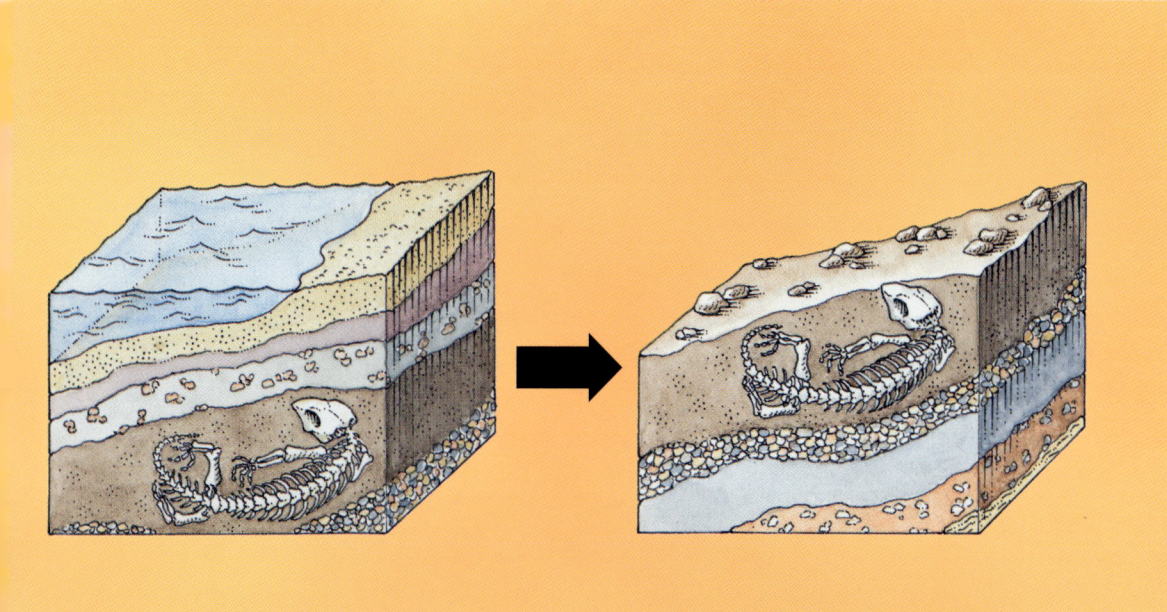

Some animals were trapped in ice. They turned into fossils.

Some animals were trapped in something sticky.
They turned into fossils, too.

11

Some animals walked in mud.
They left prints in the mud.
The prints turned into fossils.

13

14

Some plants were covered in mud. They left prints.

The prints turned into fossils, too.

Fossils tell about animals
and plants that lived long ago.